Learning from Religion

I Wonder ...

Kevin O'Donnell

Hodder & Stoughton

A MEMBER OF THE HODDER HEADLINE GROUP

Acknowledgements

The publishers would like to thank the following for their permission to reproduce material in this volume:

David Higham Associates for the extract from *Watership Down* by Richard Adams; Pan Books Ltd for the extract from *The Hitchhiker's Guide to the Galaxy* by Douglas Adams; Bible text is reproduced from the Good News Bible © American Bible Society, New York, 1966,1971 and1976 published by The Bible Societies/Harper Collins, with permission.

The lower artwork on page 30 is taken from *The Little Prince* by A Saint-Exupery.

Every effort has been made to trace and acknowledge ownership of copyright. The publishers will be glad to make suitable arrangements with any copyright holders it has not been possible to contact.

The Publishers would like to thank the following for their permission to reproduce the following copyright photographs in this volume:

Andes Press Agency (p21, p22b, p34l, p34r, p35tl, p35tr, p35bl); Bridgeman Art Library (p36, p46); Camera Press Ltd (p22t, p47r); Christine Osborne (p9); Corrymeela Community (p23); Ecoscene (p29tl, p29tr, p29b); Eye Ubiquitous (p19, 24); Frank Gordon (p9); Haags Gemeentemuseum (p42); Heather Angel (p44); Israel Government Tourist Office (p15); Jewish Education Bureau (p35br); Mel Thompson (p5, p13, p16); Minotaur Designs (p40); Mr Sharma (p33); Muhammed Ansar (p11); NASA (p4, p28, p37, p41); Sally and Richard Greenhill (p27); Science Photo Library: Dr Jeremy Burgess (p41r); Swan Photographic Agency (p16b); Taize Community (p17); Topham (p20).

Cover Photograph

The cover photograph has been supplied by NASA. It shows the satellite Io passing over the surface of Jupiter. It was taken by the spacecraft Voyager II as it passed at a distance of 8 million miles from the giant planet. Io is the most volcanically active body known in our solar system. Its orange colour is thought to be caused by deposits of sulphur from its continuous eruptions.

Compare this with the photograph of our own planet on page 28.

The immensities of space and the beauty of our environment are a great source of wonder.

British Library Cataloguing in Publication Data

O'Donnell, Kevin
I Wonder.. – (Learn about Religion)
I. title II. Series
291.07
ISBN 0 340 559 268

First published 1992
Impression number   11 10 9 8 7 6 5 4 3
Year   1999 1998 1997 1996 1995

Printed in Hong Kong for Hodder & Stoughton Educational, a dvision of Hodder Headline Plc, 338 Euston Road, London NW1 3BH by Colorcraft Ltd., Hong Kong.

Contents

Look here!

Let's start with you - underneath the school uniform, or whatever clothes you wear, you're a human being...

... in a big, wide world!

Really special things happen to us that we enjoy. These things make our lives worth living.

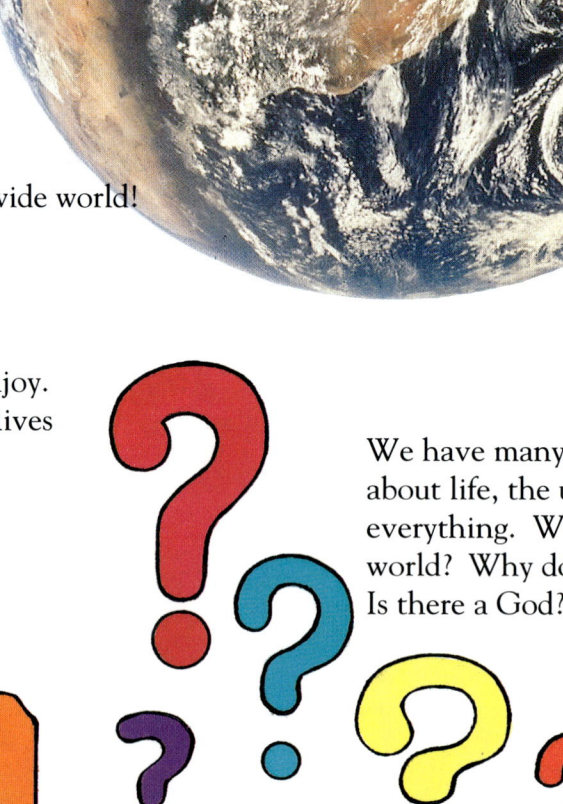

We have many questions, too, about life, the universe and everything. Why is there a world? Why do people suffer? Is there a God?... and so on.

There are different religions in the world that help to give answers to the questions we ask, and they give thanks for all the special things in life. This book will explore some of these things, and try to get you to work out how you feel about it all.

For the Teacher

This book is part of a series designed to introduce certain key concepts in RE to pupils in the final year of Primary or the first two years of Secondary school.

The book follows the spirituality approach, also known as the experiential approach.

Imagine teaching someone how to drive a car without ever giving them the chance to ride in one.

Imagine giving someone a map but never encouraging them to explore the place it describes.

Too much RE for the 10-12 age range is concerned with concrete details about books, people, buildings and rituals. We need to enter the life blood of religion and catch a hint of what it feels like to be committed or to have faith. This does not necessarily become confessional. Ninian Smart argued that the experiential was an important dimension alongside those of myth, ritual, story, doctrine, and the ethical; "... it would be foolish to think that being 'objective' means that we only look at temples, churches and the outer behaviour. We must penetrate beyond what is publicly observable. How could we give a proper account of Paul's apostolate without referring to his shattering experience on the Damascus Road?"[1]

We must not shy away from the affective side of religious belief and practice. The importance of this dimension can be seen in the Attainment in RE report [2] with its section 'Awareness of life experiences and question they raise.', and also the sections dealing with ultimate questions, worship, mediation, and celebration.

When using the term 'Spirituality' this is meant to be as inclusive as possible for State school RE. For a theist, spirituality is inseparable from a relationship with God, as is indeed the case for myself, but a non-theist is also concerned with values , awe, compassion and purpose. Some religious traditions are non-theist, such as Buddhism or Taoism. Spirituality means deep values, deep questions and deep feelings.

Exercises for the pupils are set at the bottom of each page, and suggestions for the teacher are listed at the end of the book.

Notes:

(1) Ninian Smart *The Religious Experience of Mankind* Collins 1977 p12.

(2) *Attainment in RE - a Handbook for Teachers* The Regional RE Centre (Midlands)

Some notes on Meditation and on conducting a Guided Fantasy

Meditation

The meditation techniques used in this book are neutral - they do not belong to the doctrine or practice of any particular religion. They are not the same thing as TM (Transcendental Meditation) which uses certain techniques and special mantras to be repeated, usually connected with Hinduism. No particular philosophy lies behind the use of meditation in these pages, and it is not intended to be part of 'new age' thinking, which tries to make people realise their own potential and their own 'divinity'. It does, however, follow basic relaxation techniques which are useful for relieving stress, including rhythmic breathing.

Slowing down the cognitive side of the mind and taking time to be peaceful and still is a necessary tonic in itself for Western people who are saturated with the rational, and with a fast-paced, media-rich lifestyle. It helps us to become aware of the inner life, however that is understood, and allows our imaginations to soar. Many of the meditation exercises are designed to engage both the imagination and the emotions to explore a particular topic.

The basic technique is to relax the body and regulate the breathing as follows: -

1) Sit comfortably, back and neck straight, feet firmly on the ground, hands on the lap.

2) Close eyes and count sets of ten breaths for a time. Then just breathe, but try to listen to the sound of the air entering and leaving the body.

3) It is then time for the suggestion that something is to be imagined, or that a phrase (such as, 'May I be at peace.') is repeated. Clear, short instructions should be given.

4) At the end, people should be told that the exercise is coming to an end. They should count ten breaths, and then open their eyes.

(NB In the context of chapter 9, this exercise may be likened to finding the centre of a maze.)

Guided Fantasy

Once people are relaxed and in a meditative state they can be guided through an imaginative meditation. In the meditative state, we enter, mainly, into alpha brainwaves (waking consciousness is normally beta). This is like the state on the verge of falling asleep, when we can dream very vividly, and images might pop into our minds.

After the warm up relaxation/meditation exercise, start to construct a scene, and then slowly guide people through this. The following is an example of a guided fantasy through the four seasons (see chapter 2):

- Imagine that you are out walking on a cold, winter's day. Feel the cold breeze on your face. Feel the coldness in your fingertips. Hear the grass crunching underfoot. Walk on through the woods, and watch the bare trees swaying in the wind. Think how they look like skeletons.

- You come to a stream, and you splash through this, breaking the ice. The sunlight starts to sparkle on this. You feel its gentle warmth on your face.

- Walk down the stream, watching the sunlight dance on the water. You stop and notice a flower breaking through the grass. Turn around and you see a carpet of flowers in bloom, of all colours. What colours can you see? Notice what they smell like.

- You hear birds singing, and you look up, and you have to shield your eyes from the sun. You wipe the perspiration from your brow, and shelter under a tree which is now full of green leaves. You watch squirrels darting about among the branches.

- You walk on, and you notice that you are getting more and more tired. Leaves are turning yellow and brown, and are falling around you. Hear them crunch under your feet.

- You sit down to rest, and you notice that the

colourful flowers are wilting and turning brown. The wind blows, and it is getting cold. More leaves blow from the trees, and only bare branches remain. Feel the cold breeze on your face.

- Fix your gaze on the scene before you for a few seconds. Now count ten breaths, and then open your eyes.

A debriefing time is needed. Collect feedback of what the participants felt, saw and heard in the course of the fantasy. How do they feel after the event?

Important

If you do not see the value of this type of noncognitive exercise, then I can only say 'Try it.'. Many people find it richly rewarding. If you do not, simply ignore it.

Guided Fantasies for use with other chapters in this book:

Chapter 6   A meditation on the stream of life.

- Sit comfortably, and breathe regularly.
- Count your breaths for a time.
- Start to feel all the movements of your body - breath, heart, bones, various gurglings.
- Feel the ground beneath your feet and how it supports you.
- Listen to any sounds made by birds, dogs or cats near you.
- Imagine that you are swimming in the stream of life. What other animals do you see in your mind, and what noises do you hear?
- Count breaths, and then open your eyes.

Chapter 8   A meditation of the dance of life.

- Breathe deeply and regularly and close your eyes.
- Bring to mind all the movements you have been through today from waking up until now.
- Imagine all the movements you might have throughout the rest of the day.
- Think of the movement that has gone on to make the chair you have underneath you - the life of the tree if it is wooden, or the process in the factory if it is plastic.
- Listen for the sounds outside. Think of the movement made by the things or creatures that have made those sounds.
- Count ten breaths, then open your eyes.

Chapter 9

A fantasy for this chapter could start with different parts of the body, and then ask the pupils to imagine that they are flying up above the school, above the city, above the counrty, above the Earth. They end up amidst the spinning galaxies. Then, step by step, return.

Chapter 10   A fantasy about resurrection.

- Close your eyes and breathe deeply for awhile.
- Imagine that your body is getting more and more heavy.
- You lie down and rest. Your body feels like a lump of lead.
- You start to feel a warmth in your chest, rising up into your head and down into your legs.
- You leap up and run out of the room. You join your friends, and everyone is laughing and dancing.

[Afterwards, the pupils may talk about how this felt: how they felt when they lay down and when they ran outside; what was happening outside.]

1 Who am I?

Who are you?

It seems a simple question, but we are all many people, in a way. Think of how you behave with the following people;

FRIENDS

TEACHERS

GRANDPARENTS

SHOP ASSISTANTS

THINGS TO DO

1 Go through the above list, and any other people you can think of, and write a few lines about how you behave with each one.

2 Play the 'Who are you?' game. Get into pairs, and one person asks you the question 'Who are you?' over and over again for two minutes. Answer with whatever comes into your head. At first it will be easy - your name, address, hobbies but you will soon start getting stuck! After two minutes, swop around.

One answer to the question is to list all the chemicals that make up your body. In a human being there are:

- *45 litres of water*

- *the amount of iron in a small nail*

- *enough carbon to make 9,000 pencils*

- *phosphorous for about 2,200 matches*

- *the fat from 7 bars of soap*

- *enough lime to white-wash a chicken coop*

- *plus small amounts of magnesium and sulphur.*

A person is also a thinking, feeling, living being.

THINGS TO DO

1 Working in pairs, write short drama sketches about the scene above. One of you should argue that the chemicals form a person because they are what we are all made of. The other should argue that there is more to us than that.

2 Think about times when you have been very joyful, sad, excited and frightened. We all have strong feelings as living persons; talk about some of these as a class.

These people are taking part in a Mardi Gras parade. This happens on the Tuesday before the start of the Christian season of Lent. It is a final party before a time of self denial. The people wear masks until midnight.

People wear masks because they want to hide their identity. In the Mardi Gras, people do not want anyone to know who they are when they are partying. Some criminals wear masks so that they will not be recognised - bankrobbers, or highwaymen in the past. We have comic book stories of masked heroes and villains.

In early times, and in some tribal societies today, people believed that they would gain the power of the person whose mask they wore. Wearing the mask of the rain god would bring control over the weather, for example.

We act differently with different people, and this is like wearing different masks.

These are 'masks' that we might wear to cover up how we really feel.

Think of a time when you were afraid to let someone know what you really felt.

THINGS TO DO

Making masks

1 Place your hand over your face and stretch it out. then place it on a piece of card and draw a face shape around it.

2 Design two different masks, one on the back of the other. One is to be how you would like others to see you. The other is how you see yourself.

Mandala Patterns

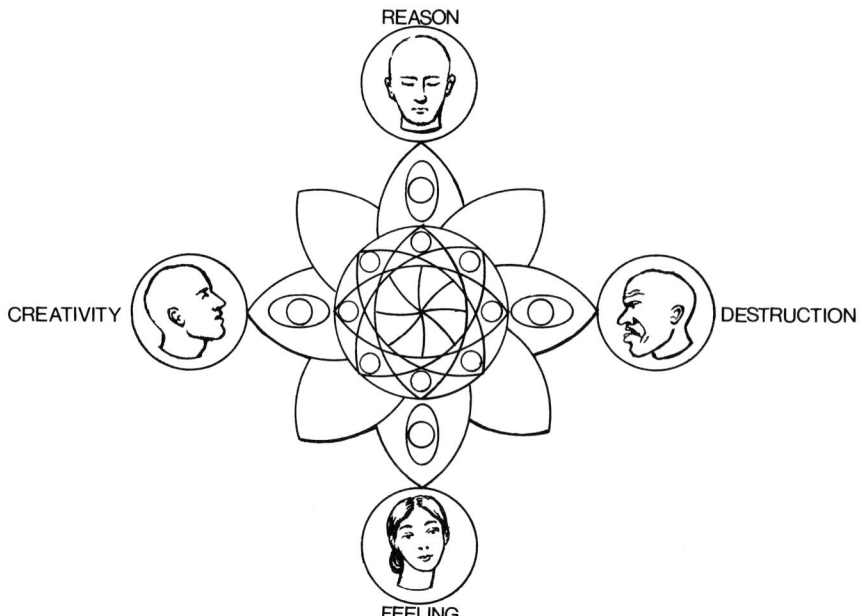

A *mandala* is a picture of what you are inside. Different objects link together into a pattern. Many mandalas have four points, balancing each other out. In the drawing above, our creative power is set against our destructive power, and our power to reason, to think, is set against the strength of our feelings. These should all balance inside us. There are examples below of what can happen if they are out of balance.

A mandala can have any number of points - another common type has three points, like a triangle.

In the above pattern, three forces in our lives are shown. Something starts, comes to an end, and something new comes in its place. The acorn grows into an oak, the oak dies, but leaves many more acorns.

THINGS TO DO

1 Design a mandala with four points. Choose four feelings, or forces, that you think are at work in you.

2 Design a mandala with three points. Think of a time when something ends, and then something new starts, perhaps losing a friend and making a new one. Draw pictures of this at each point of the mandala.

3 Draw an outline of a figure like the one below, and draw in any sorts of people (heroes and villains) or ideas that you think you have inside your personality.

INSIDE ME THERE IS...

10

The Amrit Ceremony

Some races, and some religions, have special ceremonies which young people go through to show that they are adults. They leave their childhood behind, and take on new responsibilities in their families, and in the community.

Young Sikhs go through the Amrit ceremony. This dates back to one of their founders, Guru Gobind Singh. He gave them a special ceremony to show that they were one people, with one faith.

Amrit is a mixture of sugar and water, and Sikhs go through a type of baptism to show that they are true disciples. When they do this, they become members of the Khalsa, 'the pure ones'.

Those who join the Khalsa must not take tobacco or drugs, and must not cut their hair. Sikh men have to wear these five things: a comb for keeping their hair clean and tidy (Kangha); long hair and beard (Kesh); shorts worn as underclothes (Kachs); a steel bracelet (Kara); a short sword (Kirpan).

The candidates kneel in front of the holy book, in a way that shows they are ready for action. Notice that they are not wearing any shoes - this is to show respect for the place of worship.

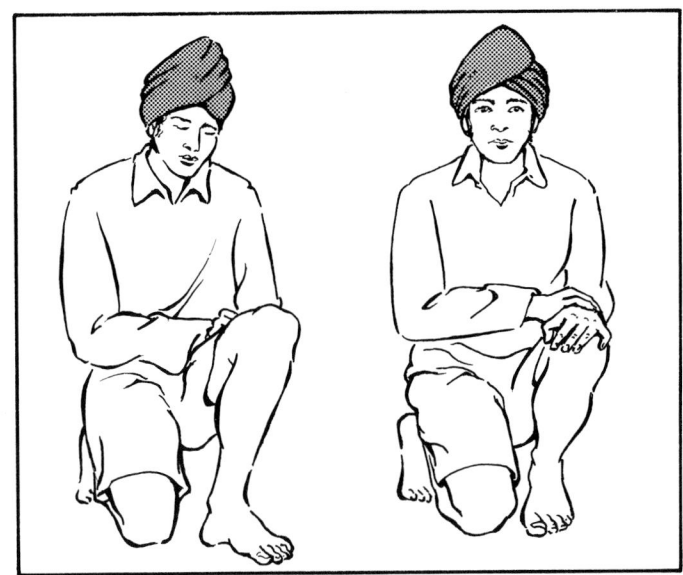

The candidates then drink a little of the Amrit, after saying this prayer, 'The Khalsa is of God and the Victory is of God." This action is repeated five times, and then the Amrit is sprinkled over the eyes five times, and over the head. The Mool Mantra is then said by everyone:

There is one God; His name is truth,

The all pervading Creator,

Without fear, without hatred;

Immortal, unborn, self-existent.

THINGS TO DO

1   Do young people in this country have any ceremonies that show that they have left childhood behind? Think up a ceremony that could be used.

2   Why do you think sugar and water is used in the Amrit ceremony?

3   Draw a picture strip showing the different stages in the Amrit ceremony.

4   Write an imaginary entry for a Sikh boy's diary, describing what happened to him at the Amrit ceremony, and saying how he felt.

11

2 Journeying

We all go on journeys - the trip to school, your family going to work, the summer holiday, going shopping on a Saturday. We walk, we run, we cycle, we take a bus or a train, we drive in a car, we fly in an aeroplane, or sail in a ship.

Stop and think... How many journeys have you made today? What about the rest of your family?

Some journeys are exciting, and are planned well in advance, such as going on holiday.

Think about the last holiday you went on. How long before it did your family start planning? What did you have to get ready?

Some journeys are sad, but mixed with happiness. If you ever moved house you will know what this is like. You pack up all your things and leave the house and your friends behind, but you are going on to a new place, where you will meet new people.

THINGS TO DO

1 Draw a map of your journey to school.

2 Fill two sides of paper with items to do with your last holiday - photographs, brochures, maps, tickets, and a few lines describing it in your own words.

3 If you have not had a holiday for some time, then try to write a few lines saying why you miss having one.

4 Talk, as a class, about experiences of moving home.

5 Working in groups, design a collage about journeying include all the different forms of transport.

Abram's Journey - a story from the Hebrew Bible

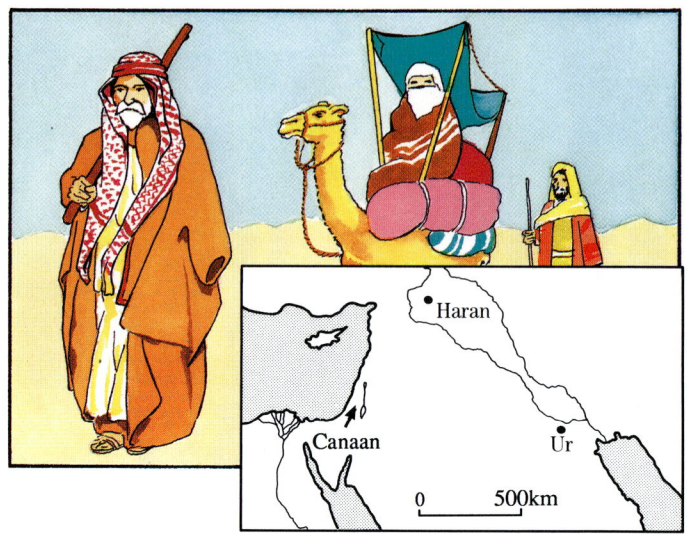

The Bible story of Abram involves him leaving his homeland. He takes his family and their belongings, and sets out, not sure of where he is going. He is searching for a land to settle in, and descendants. In the story, God tells him to set out, and he has enough faith, enough trust, to do so.

'The Lord said to Abram, "Leave your country, your relatives, and your father's home, and go to a land that I am going to show you. I will give you many descendants, and they will become a great nation. I will bless you and make your name famous, so that you will be a blessing . . . ."'

'When Abram was seventy-five years old, he started out from Haran, as the Lord had told him to do, and Lot went within him. Abram took his wife, Sara, his nephew Lot, and all his wealth and all the slaves they had acquired in Haran, and they started out for the land of Canaan.'

THINGS TO DO

1 Talk as a class about how you would feel if you had to leave your home and most things that you owned.

2 Read through the story of Abram. Have you ever had to go somewhere new or do something that you had never done before? What did you feel like? Talk in pairs about this.

The Seasons

Spring

New life begins to stir in Spring. The cold, winter weather has gone, and the sun's warmth is felt on the earth.

Summer

The summer is a time of long days and bright sunshine. We feel hot and lazy, and don't feel like working very much. It is the holiday season, and the trees are heavy with fruit, and the flowers are all in bloom.

Autumn

Autumn is like old age. Crops ripen in the fields. Then plants begin to wilt and die

Winter

Winter is like death for most things in nature. Plants die, some animals hibernate, the trees stand like bare skeletons, and the cold weather bites hard.

An old story

The seasons were a mystery to ancient people, and they were frightened that the spring would not come back again. Then things would not grow, and they could not eat, or have any warmth!

The ancient Greeks told a story to try and explain why the autumn and the winter came, and the crops died.

Persephone, the daughter of the Earth Goddess, Demeter, was given in marriage to the Lord of the Underworld, Pluto. The agreement was that she would spend six months underground with Pluto, and six on the earth with her mother.

Persephone returning to the earth.

THINGS TO DO

1. Write a poem about spring or about winter

2. Write a few paragraphs, imagining that you area person living in ancient times when the winter time came. What would you have felt like?

3. Act out the story of Pluto and Persephone in groups.

4. How do we explain the coming and going of the seasons, today?

The Journey of Life

Life is like a journey we start out at birth, grow up, grow old, and end at death.

The journey of life is like the journey through the seasons - spring is like childhood, summer like adulthood, autumn is like old age, and winter is like dying.

THINGS TO DO

1   Draw a line across a piece of paper; it should go right off one end of the paper.

   • The start of this represents your date of birth. Write this on the line.

   • Mark along the line important events that have happened to you, or things that you remember very well. They might be happy or sad. You may draw small pictures to go with these.

   • Make sure that you leave some of the line blank, because that stands for the things that are going to happen in the future!

2   Talk, as a class, about the things you have given up, or changed, because you are growing older and you are no longer young children. Have you found this easy?

3   What things do you forward to when you grow older? What things frighten you?

4   Draw a journey of life, showing the four different stages.

5   Write a few lines about what you think you will be like, and what you will be doing, when you are an adult.

A Pilgrimage to Jerusalem

Religions have special places of pilgrimage. These are holy places, connected with the founders of their faith, or with a special experience of God. Poeple travel to them to seek to be closer to God. Jerusalem is a holy city to three of the world's faiths, Judaism, Christianity and Islam. A pilgrimage is a journey to a special place, to show that you are serious about your faith. It also reminds the believer that life is a journey from birth to death, from God to God.

Ibrahim is from Cowley, in East Oxford. He has come with his family to visit the holy places of his faith, Islam. He visits the Dome of the Rock, a mosque. This is built upon a rock where the Prophet Muhammad is believed to have journeyed to heaven. Ibrahim's heart misses a beat when he looks at this place; the prophet whom he honours once stood here!

Jonathan's family are from Manchester. They are members of the Jewish faith. They visit the Western Wall, the only part of their old Temple that is still standing after the Roman Soldiers destroyed it in 70CE. They stop there and say their prayers, sometimes leaving a written prayer in the cracks in the wall. *It feels very powerful to touch these old stones.* This wall is sometimes called 'The Wailing Wall' because of the prayers said there, and sadness at the destruction of the Temple.

Angela is from Bracknell, Berkshire. She is a Christian, a member of the Roman Catholic Church. She has come with her family on a tour of the Israel. She is visiting the Holy Sepulchre, the tomb where many people think Jesus was buried before he rose again. It feels quiet, peaceful and very mysterious.

THINGS TO DO

1 Consult an atlas and work out how many miles Jerusalem is from England. Why do religious believers bother to make such a journey?

2 Ask a Travel Agent for some brochures about Israel and Jerusalem. Make a small brochure yourself. Draw pictures and stick on some photographs. Describe the main attractions.

3 Imagine you are Ibrahim or Angela. Write a few lines about what you see and how you feel.

4 Think of a prayer that you might want to leave at the Western Wall - perhaps for world peace - and write it out. You may want to put these into slots in large sheets of sugar paper and display them, like a small 'Wailing Wall'.

3 It's Amazing! - the experience of wonder

Sometimes we can be surprised by a beautiful scene; something takes our breath away and makes us stop and look. It is joyful and refreshing, lifting our spirits. We are surprised by joy.

A brilliant sunrise or sunset, filling the clouds with colour, or a rushing stream in the sunlight, can catch our attention.

This is the experience of wonder. ('Wonder' does not mean 'to think about', here, but something that is 'wonderful', full of wonder!) It is beautiful, breathtaking and amazing. We feel overcome in its presence.

ancient beauty - they have been there for millions of years! As we look up, we can feel very small. Who are we, tiny creatures, in this vast universe? We feel overcome.

Small things can catch our attention, too, like the beautiful pattern of a spider's web, or a brilliantly coloured dragonfly darting across a stream.

Sometimes we might stare up at the night sky and look at all the thousands of stars. They shine and twinkle on a black velvet background. There is

To wonder is to be amazed, to have your breath taken away by a thing's beauty, or age, or size.

THINGS TO DO

1 Have you had an experience of wonder like the ones mentioned here?

2 Have you heard about any other experiences of wonder?

3 Watch the video 'The Snowman' by Raymond Briggs. Can you see any scenes of wonder in that? Talk about this as a class.

4 Write a few lines, imagining that you are the first person to set foot on Mars. How might it feel? (Perhaps you could watch a scene from the moonlanding on the Pathe News Video for 1969 - this would give you an idea of a person's feelings when stepping onto a new planet.)

16

Wonder in Worship

The Taizé community in central France is a monastery for men belonging to all the different Christian churches - Roman Catholic, Anglican, Methodist, Lutheran, and so on. It began in 1940, as a place of prayer for all nations.

All during the summer months people come to stay for at least a week at a time, mainly from Europe, but also from India, the Phillipines, from Africa and elsewhere. Several thousand people will be staying at the height of the season in August. Most are young, in their teens or early twenties.

There are Bible studies and discussion groups as well as three services of prayer and praise with the brothers.

The Church is full of atmosphere, with people singing in different languages, and times of complete silence. Modern, simple songs are sung rather than long hymns. They are learnt quickly and repeated over and over, such as:

> In the Lord I'll be ever thankful,
> In the Lord I will rejoice.
> Look to him, do not be afraid,
> In him rejoicing, the Lord is near.

On Saturday nights, small candles are held by everyone, and as one is lit, the light is passed along the rows until the whole place is ablaze with light. The altar at the front of the church always has dozens of flickering candles on it and around it.

The Music, the quiet, and the candle light, all seem so beautiful and take your breath away. Brother Roger, the founder, hopes this place will help different races to make friends with each other - Taizé is to be a place of forgiveness and welcome for all.

THINGS TO DO

1 Find Taizé on a map of France. Which large town is it near?

2 Look at the large photograph at the top of the page. How do you think you would feel if you were there?

3 Why was Taizé started, and by whom?

4 Listen in classs to a tape of Taizé songs - or watch a video, such as 'Taizé, that little springtime'. How do they make you feel? (For more information about Taizé, contact Taizé Community, F-71250, Taizé, Cluny, France.)

'Holy, Holy, Holy' - a story from the Bible

The prophet Isaiah lived in the eighth century BCE. In the year 740BCE King Uzziah of Jerusalem died, and one day, when Isaiah was praying in the Temple, he felt overwhelemd by a presence.

Worship in the Temple would have been breathtaking. There were the glittering gold and silver ornaments. There were flickering oil lamps, and clouds of burning incense. The priests wore long, colourful robes and the Psalms were sung with the accompaniment of musical instruments such as the trumpet and the cymbals. Isaiah felt that all of this took his breath away, and in the beauty of it all, he sensed God's presence. The Bible story says that he had a vision something only he saw in his mind.

> 'In the year that King Uzziah died, I saw the Lord. He was sitting on his throne, high and exalted, and his robe filled the whole Temple. Round him flaming creatures were standing, each of which had six wings. Each creature covered its face with two wings, and its body with two, and used the other two for flying. They were calling out to each other:
>
> "Holy, Holy, Holy
> The Lord Almighty is holy!
> His glory fills the world."
>
> The sound of their voices made the foundations of the Temple shake, and the temple itself was filled with smoke..'
>
> (Isaiah 6:1-4)

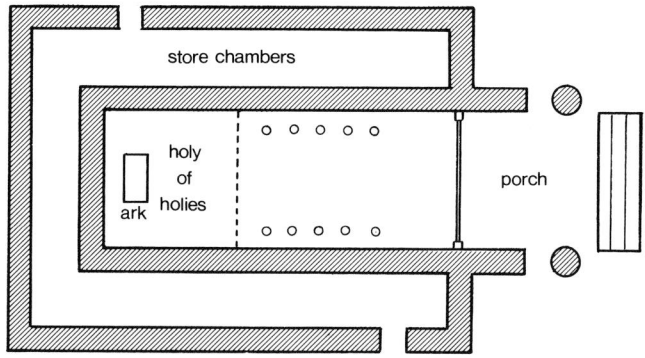

The temple as is would have been in Isaiah's time. Only the High Priest could go into the Holy of Holies.

THINGS TO DO

1 Try to draw or paint the vision of Isaiah, with the strange, winged, flaming creatures.

2 How do you think Isaiah felt? Read the rest of the story in Isaiah 6. Have you ever felt that you lhave been in the presence of something holy?

3 Read about the first meeting with the elves in J.R.R.Tolkien's, *The Lord of the Rings* (Book 1 'The Fellowship of the Ring'). Does anything there make you feel full of wonder? Is there anything that feels religious about the elves?

You're one of a kind!

There is something wonderful about each person. When you stop to think about it, it is amazing! There is only one of you.

There has never, ever, been anyone else the same as you, there is not now, and there never will be. You're one of a kind.

There is a special word for things that there is just one of - we say that they are 'unique'.

People are formed in their mother's womb from material from their father and mother, from 'genes'. The mixture given to each person is unique: everyone is different and special in some way.

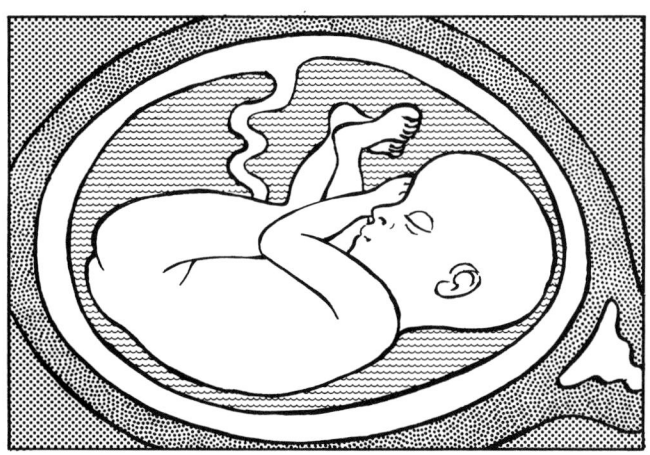

You might be like your parents and the rest of your family in some ways, but there is still something different and individual about you. You are you, and not them.

If a work of art is unique, then it is very hard to say what it is worth. To say that something is 'priceless' means that you cannot put a price on it. It is worth too much. It is too special.

Human beings are like that, too!

THINGS TO DO

1 Why are human beings like priceless works of art?

2 Make a chart of all the things that are similar and different between you and your family.

3 Make a poster of 'yourself' - perhaps you can stick a photo of yourself on it, and draw around it the things that you like doing.

4 Making Friends - the experience of forgiveness

East and West Berlin used to be separated by a wall that was built by the communist government of East Germany in the 1960s. This was opened up in 1989, and demolished in 1990. The two sides had become friends, and Germany was soon reunited into one country. People celebrated and danced on the wall when they knew it was going to come down.

A relationship can be broken by many things. there is a disagreement, and anger erupts. Perhaps one person acted very selfishly and hurt the other. To make friends again, we have to forgive and forget. This is not always easy. Pride can stop us. It is hard to own up and admit that we were at fault.

If we have been hurt, it is hard to let go of our anger and hurt. That is what forgiveness is - letting go of wrong feelings. Bearing a grudge against someone can work away within us and fill us with worry and bitterness. We are not so nice to know, then!

Once we have let go and forgiven someone, we might get to know them in a much deeper way. A real and lasting friendship can develop sometimes because you have opened up to each other, 'warts and all'. You might learn new things about yourself.

Some things hurt very deeply, and these might take a long time to forgive. It is said that time can be a great healer! This is particularly true of people who are hurt in wars, and who lose loved ones. If we cannot forgive, our feelings get bottled up inside, and cannot flow as freely as they should.

THINGS TO DO

1 What does it mean to 'forgive'?

2 Draw two pictures of the Berlin Wall; one of soldiers patrolling with machine guns and shooting at someone trying to cross, and one of the people celebrating on it.

3 Have you ever been frightened that you were about to be punished for doing something wrong, but then you were let off, so long as it did not happen again? What did this feel like?

4 Can you think of some things that would be very hard to forgive?

Stories about Forgiveness

The Lost Son

Jesus told a story about a father who had two sons. One asked for his share of the money that his father was going to leave him when he died.

He took it, and left home, and went to a distant country. He spent it without a thought for his future. He drank too much, and held parties, and attracted lots of friends.

One day, he ran out of money, and all his friends left him. They wanted his riches, and did not like him for himself.

Now very poor, he had to take a job helping to feed pigs, and when a famine came to the land, he had to eat some things thrown out for them!

Suddenly he realised how stupid he had been. He could have been at home, enjoying life on his father's farm.

Perhaps he should go back. His father would be too disgusted to take him back as his son, but he might hire him as a worker. He journeyed back, and when his father saw him returning, he rushed out and hugged him. He forgave him, welcomed him back, and threw a party.

THINGS TO DO

1 How do you react to the story of the Lost Son? Do you think the father was being 'soft'? Why did he not chase after his son to bring him back? Why did he wait until he had come to his senses?

2 Divide into groups, and retell this story set in modern times. Then each group can act out its version in front of the class.

The Tunnel - *a Japanese Buddhist story*

Zenkai fell in love with his employer's wife and when he was found out, he killed his master. The couple fled far away, and lived as thieves. Eventually, Zenkai quarrelled with her, and they separated. Zenkai wandered about, until one day he decided to do a good deed to try to make up for having killed his employer.

He knew of a dangerous road that went over a cliff. Many people had been killed there, and so he set about digging a tunnel through the mountain. After thirty years the tunnel was 2,280 feet long, 20 feet high and 30 feet wide.

Two years before the tunnel was finished, his employer's son found Zenkai in the tunnel and threatened to kill him. Zenkai offered to give up his life, but begged him to let him finish off the tunnel first. The son agreed, and camped nearby. Eventually, he was so fed up with waiting that he joined in the digging. When the tunnel was finished Zenkai said, "Now you can cut off my head."

The young man bowed his head, with tears in his eyes, and said, "How can I cut off my own teacher's head?"

THINGS TO DO

1 Why do you think the young man refused to kill Zenkai?

2 Why did the young man call Zenkai his 'teacher'?

3 Draw a comic strip telling the story.

4 Make up your own story about two people forgiving one another.

The Peacemaker - Mahatma Gandhi

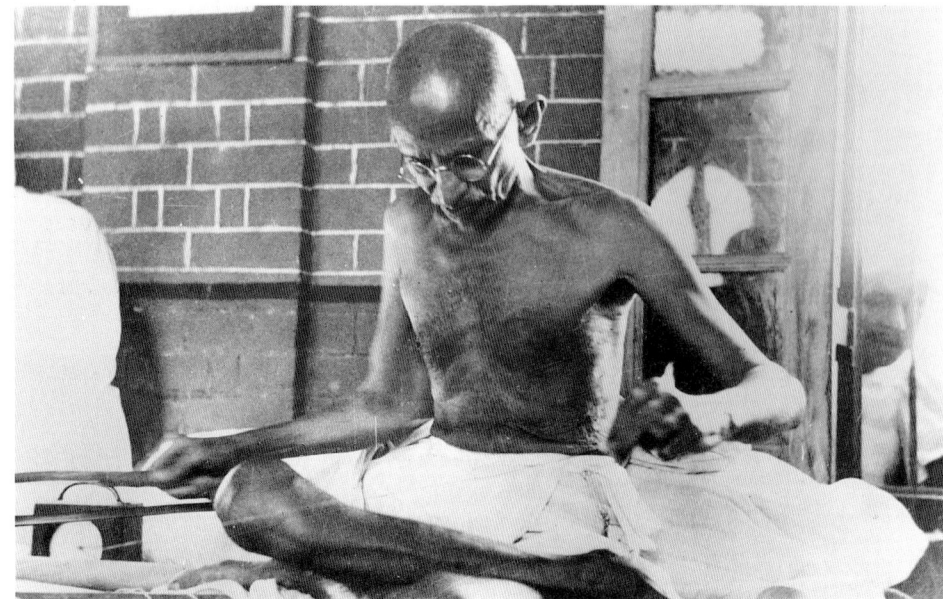

Gandhi tried to teach Indian villages to be self-sufficient by spinning their own cotton (They had been using cotton imported from Lancashire!) and he spun his own cotton on his own wheel. The Indian flag still has a picture of a spinning wheel upon it.

Mohandas Gandhi, called 'Mahatma' (Great Soul), is one of the great heroes of India. He was a Hindu who supported his country's struggle for freedom from British rule (India gained independence in 1947) but he opposed the use of violence. He supported ahimsa, non-violent protest - marches, 'sit-ins' writing articles, making speeches, and organising prayer meetings for the different faiths represented in India. Hindus and Muslims often fought each other, and wanted rights and land of their own. Gandhi encouraged them to respect one another as children of the One God. He organised ashrams, communes, where different groups and faiths lived and worked together, including the lowest class of Indian society, the 'Untouchables', who were very poor. Indian society had very strict levels of class called castes. Gandhi renamed the Untouchables the 'Harijan', the 'Children of God' and campaigned for more rights for them. This made him unpopular with the rich castes!

Many pray about troubles in the world, as in the picture below. Prayers were offered to try to prevent war in the Gulf. People feel that this makes them feel better, that they have done something, at least. It is not a magic formula, but a way of sharing deep feelings and hopes. Believers feel that offering things to God can strengthen them to do something about a problem, and help the people being prayed for, too.

THINGS TO DO

1   Divide a page into four, and draw four things that Gandhi did to help people. Write a sentence by each one.

2   Do you think we should always follow Gandhi's advice and not use any violence? What about the Second World War, or the war in the Gulf? Have a classroom discussion about this.

3   Write a prayer for peace in the world. Perhaps some of these could be read out in assembly.

Making Friends in Northern Ireland -
the work of the Corrymeela community

The worship centre, open to all Christians, is called the Croi (Gaelic for 'heart'). The prayer of St Francis of Assisi is engraved on the glass doors of the Croi:

Lord make me an instrument of your peace,
Where there is hatred let me sow love...

A Corrymeela poem described the Croi in this way:

The Croi is like an ear,
A great intricate ear to catch prayers in.
It is a trumpet wound round
Into a winding horn for sounding praise
For heralding good news...

The Corrymeela centre was opened in 1965 as a place for learning, worship, and for peace and quiet for people from different Christian churches. 'Corrymeela' means 'Hill of Harmony' in Gaelic, and the community is based in a small village, with different types of buildings, on a cliff on County Antrim's north coast.

Northern Ireland has many troubles and different groups fight each other. It is too simplistic to say that it is all about religion, about Roman Catholics against Protestants. It is also about politics. Some (called 'Unionists' or 'Loyalists') want Northern Ireland to remain part of Great Britain. Others (called 'Nationalists' or 'Republicans') want a united Ireland.

The British army patrols Northern Ireland, and violence often breaks out in certain areas, though this land is beautiful and most people want to live in peace. Corrymeela tries to bring different groups together, to allow Irish Protestants and Catholics to meet. People come to Corrymeela for worship, teaching, for some peace and quiet away from everyday life, and for concerts and games.

Up to 160 people can stay at Corrymeela at any one time. Tensions are relaxed as they play and pray together, share food and do the washing up!

The Corrymeela cross shows four triangles meeting around a cross. This represents different groups and different points of view meeting around faith in Christ.

The message of Corrymeela is perhaps summed up in the words of folk-singer Tom Paxton:

Peace, Peace will, Peace will come. Let it begin with me.

THINGS TO DO

1   Why is there trouble in Northern Ireland?

2   What is Corrymeela doing to bring forgiveness in Northern Ireland?

3   What is the worship centre called, and why?

4   Why do you think the worship centre is compared to 'an ear to catch prayers in'? What does this mean?

5   Make a Corrymeela cross by drawing a cross in the centre of a large sheet of paper, and then placing photographs and drawings around it in the shape of four triangles. Use pictures of different groups of people, such as young people and elderly people, the rich and the poor.

5 Love Is ...

Love is a four letter word! It is a word we hear all the time. What do we mean by it?

Write down as many ideas as you can for "Love is..."

By love, we often mean romance. We think of blushes, and holding hands, kisses and strong feelings for someone else.

Sometimes people might talk about loving someone as a friend - then we mean *liking* someone.

Sometimes we mean something stronger by 'love'. We mean caring for people who need us, by putting ourselves out for them. Like visiting a sick relative in hospital...

Or, perhaps, when someone gives blood as blood donor.

Or a parent getting up at night to calm a crying child... It might be something very costly, even to the point of giving your life for someone else.

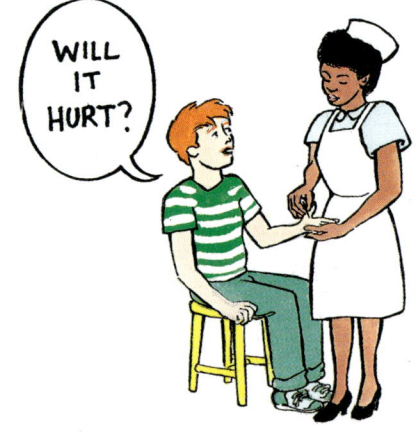

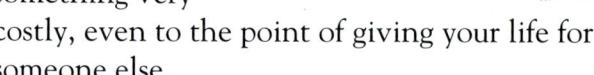

Girl Dies Trying To Save Toddler From Speeding Car...

THINGS TO DO

1 Think of an example of romantic love, friendly love, and costly love. Draw a picture for each of these, and write about them.

2 Think about a time when you felt cared for. Write a few lines about this.

3 Watch out in newspapers or magazines for an example of costly love, and bring this into the class.

The Story of St Alban

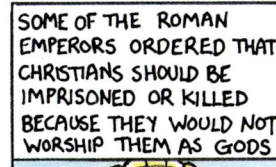

THINGS TO DO

1 Find out what Verulamium is called today.

2 What sort of love does the story of Alban show us?

3 Read *John 15:12-14*. How might this have inspired Alban?

4 Imagine that you are one of Alban's friends. You are amazed at what he has done. Write a letter to him in prison, urging him to give up his new faith. Write a reply from Alban, saying why he is behaving in this way.

Mother Teresa

Mother Teresa founded the order of Roman Catholic sisters, the Missionaries of Charity, after working for some years in Calcutta, India. Her sisters help out in the poorest part of the city where many people are homeless, living on the streets. Her sisters take in the sick and the dying, giving them comfort and care. They do not seek to convert them to Christianity, but just to show them love, even if they are at the end of their lives.

One story about Mother Teresa shows the power of the love that radiates from her. Early in her work, she was offered a disused Hindu temple to use for the care of the sick. Some of the locals feared that she was trying to convert them, and shouted insults and threw stones. A Hindu priest stopped them; "This is a living god, and not one of stone, that is walking amongst us" he said.

Another story is about a young boy who was found half - buried in a rubbish tip, covered in sores and bitten by rats. He had been left for dead, but someone had warned the Sisters and their helpers that he was there. They dug and dug and found him, barely alive. He was nursed back to health, and some months later, he called a helper over to him, and showed him a hole in his T-shirt. "This is no good!" he complained!

THINGS TO DO

1 Imagine that you are a newspaper reporter visiting the Sisters in Calcutta. Describe the work they do.

2 How do you react to the story of the boy found in the rubbish, who then complained about his T-shirt? Think about the special things in our lives that we often take for granted.

A Muslim 'Father Teresa'?

Abdus Sattar Edhi is nicknamed 'Father Teresa' in Pakistan because of his work with the poor. Mr Edhi, and his wife, Bilquis, run a charitable organisation in Karachi that provides an ambulance service four times as large as the state's, and a series of orphanages and clinics. The ambulances are on the scene whenever there is fighting between different races or religions.

The orphanages are important because some women are far too poor to look after their babies, and they are often abandoned on the streets. Bilquis leaves baskets outside her houses with messages attached, asking mothers to leave their children there. They are then raised in the orphanages.

Mr Edhi is particularly concerned with the people abandoned during the night. He and his helpers often have to take in dead bodies. His latest project is to have clinics and ambulance centres along Pakistan's highways, because driving there can often be very dangerous.

His inspiration comes from his faith, and from the teaching in the Qur'an, the Muslim holy book, to love God and neighbour.

> Have you seen someone who rejects religion? That is the person who pushes the orphan aside and does not encourage feeding the needy. (Sura 107:13)
>
> God commands justice, kindness and giving (Sura 16:90)

THINGS TO DO

1 "God commands justice, kindness and giving..." How do Abdus and Bilquis Edhi try to follow this saying in the Qur'an?

2 Imagine you are a mother about to leave her baby in one of Bilquis' baskets. Write a short note saying why you are doing this.

Care in the Community

The Elderly

Some Elderly people who live alone, feel lonely, and find it hard to manage because they have not got the strength they once had. Our bodies grow tired and weaker as we grow older.

Home helps visit some people to see that they are well, to clean and tidy, and to do their shopping.

Other elderly people live in special flats called sheltered accommodation. They have their own flats, and are very private but there is ususally a warden living nearby who will come and help if they are in need.

A common problem is that when a person starts to loose their strength, they will fall over easily, and they might not be able to pull themselves up. There will be alarm systems in the flats so that they can call for help.

Others who are too weak to look after themselves will live in a Home for the Elderly. There will be various helpers and nurses on duty there throughout the day.

The Homeless

Large cities have a problem with homeless people. These are not just elderly vagrants who have fallen on hard times; many of them are young people. Perhaps they have run away from home because they are being beaten and cruelly treated, or perhaps they have come to the cities looking for work. They find that they cannot get a job and they cannot claim Unemployment Benefit unless they have a regular address, a place to stay. They are forced to live on the streets, begging for money. They sleep in 'cardboard cities', collections of people sleeping in carboard boxes.

Another problem is that some mentally disturbed people have been encouraged to try to live in the community, rather than being kept in a special home. This has not worked for many people; they simply cannot cope, and they sleep rough, unable to hold down a job.

The problems are deep, and will take new plans and laws to solve, but various groups try to help. The 'Soup Run' is where charitable organisations such as the Salvation Army drive around giving free tea, soup and blankets. They also run a number of short stay hostels.

THINGS TO DO

1 Why do many young people find themselves out on the streets of our big cities?

2 On a piece of paper, draw a picture of your home. Think of all the things this gives you warmth, shelter, and so forth, and write these around it.

3 You may want to organise a fundraising event for one of the charities that help homeless people. Perhaps you could set up a large cardboard box in the School Hall and sponsor people to stay in it for set periods of time.

6 Spaceship Earth

The planet earth, as seen from space is a globe alive with colour - white and grey cloud, green, brown and blue tones. It is a spinning world full of life, but it is just one planet out of thousands of others moving about in the blackness of space.

This is the world that we live on; it sustains us and feeds us. We are living on a large 'spaceship' in outer space. We live on Spaceship Earth!

Human beings are just a part of the stream of life, that surrounds us and flows through us. All living things from insects to humans are connected, and all things depend upon the planet for their life.

The stream of life

Human beings are part of the stream of life, but we stand out from other creatures in some ways. We have the power of reason - we are intelligent beings able to think for ourselves. We have self-awareness - we know who we are. We have dexterity - our fingers and thumbs can make and use complicated tools. These skills give us control over our world - for better or for worse

Some other animals have intelligence - whales, dolphins, apes and dogs, for example. We are able to think enough about things and put them into practice because our bodies, standing upright, with hands that have thumbs. We have power and, rather than caring for the world we live in, humans can often be very selfish.

In a human being, endowed as we are with self-awareness, the whole universe reflects upon itself and celebrates its own wonderful journey.

(Sean McDonagh, *To Care for the Earth*)

THINGS TO DO

1 Imagine that you are an astronaut going into orbit for the first time. Try to describe what you think the earth would look like beneath you.

2 Produce a huge painting of the earth as seen from space, as a class. Work in groups of four or five on a section of the picture and assemble them along the wall afterwards.

3 Design a poster, using drawings or cutout photographs, showing the stream of life.

Earthwatch!

The selfishness of human beings shows in the destruction of the world's rainforests. These provide shelter and food for many different types of wild life, and they supply large amonts of our oxygen. They are being cut down to provide land for cattle farming and to grow crops to feed them. The meat is sold at a profit and some people become rich.

The trees do not grow back, and the loose soil cannot be used for growing crops for very long. We are thus losing many species and plants - some plants are very useful to chemists to find new medicines, too.

The 'Greenhouse Effect' means that there are more gasses in our atmosphere that trap the sun's heat. The destruction of the rainforests is helping to reduce the amount of carbon dioxide that is turned into oxygen by the trees; carbon dioxide is also pushed into the atmosphere from car exhausts. Cows produce methane, and as more people eat more meat (with an expanding fastfood industry as well) more cattle are farmed. Various items, such as aerosol sprays, contain CFCs - Chlorofluorocarbons - trap the sun's heat and also help to destroy the ozone layer which is a vital gas in the atmosphere for life to exist.

We have hunted some species to near extinction to use their meat,

or hides, or even parts of their bodies like rhino horns or elephants' tusks. Whales and dolphins are particularly under threat, not only from hunters, but also from intensive methods of fishing where large nets trap and drown the mammals (who actually breathe air though they live in the sea).

THINGS TO DO

1 Find out more about rainforests and the wildlife that lives in them. Design a poster, or write a poem about them.

2 Design a leaflet explaining the Greenhouse Effect and showing people how to avoid making it worse.

Stories about Caring for the World

The following story is taken from *The Little Prince* by Antoine De Saint-Exupery. The prince lives alone on a small planet and he goes visiting neighbouring planets, meeting interesting people.

Now there were some terrible seeds on the planet that was the home of the little prince; and these were the seeds of the baobab. The soil of the planet was infested with them. A baobab is something you will never, never be able to get rid of if you attend to it too late. It spreads over the entire planet. It bores clean through it with its roots. And if the planet is too small, and the baobabs are too many, they split it in pieces...

"it's a question of discipline", the little prince said to me later on. "When you've finished your toilet in the morning, then its time to attend to the toilet of our planet, just so, with the greatest of care. You must see to it that you pull up regularly all the baobabs...

"Sometimes," he added, "there is no harm in putting off a piece of work until another day. But when it is a matter of baobabs, that always means a catastrophy. I knew a planet that was inhabited by a very lazy man. He neglected three little bushes..."

So, as the little prince described it to me, I have made a drawing of that planet...

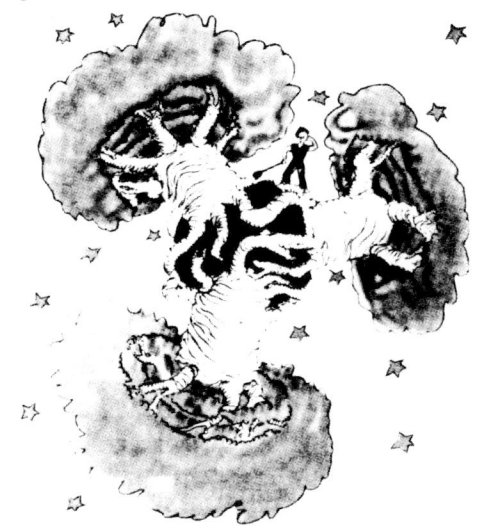

The Lazy Sons

Once there was a very hard working farmer who had two lazy sons. They did nothing to help on his land, or in the vineyards. They wasted his money and fooled around.

As the farmer grew older, he became frightened that his sons would let his farm go to ruin when he died. Years passed, and as he was dying, he called his sons to his side and told them a secret.

"Somewhere in this land I have hidden a great treasure," he said. "You will have to search and search for it, but when you find it, that will be your inheritance."

The farmer died, and the two sons started to search. They dug here and there, and pulled up the weeds. They harvested the crops and what they could not eat, they sold at the market. Gradually, they made a great deal of money from this, but still they searched and searched for the treasure. They did not find it.

One day, as they were tending the vines, one of the sons stopped and smiled. "I know where our father's treasure is," he said. "It is all around us!"

THINGS TO DO

1 What is the moral of the story from *The Little Prince?*

2 What things do we have in our world like the baobabs?

3 What sort of things have we been polluting or hurting our world with, too?

THINGS TO DO

1 What was the treasure that the farmer left to his sons?

2 How hard do you think it is to see the treasure we have all around us when we live in large cities and get our food in packs from the supermarket?

3 Try to make up a story of your own about caring for the world.

Religious Stories about Caring for the World

A Christian Story

The Christian saint, Francis of Assisi, lived from 1182-1226CE. He was known as a man of deep peace and holiness who was thought to be very close to God. A story is told about him meeting a fierce wolf in Gubbio, Italy.

The wolf had attacked and killed many people, and the citizens were afraid to leave their city unarmed. Francis went outside the city with a companion and the wolf ran to attack them with its jaws open. Francis stood his ground and made the sign of the cross. The wolf closed its jaws and stopped its charge. Francis spoke to the wolf:

"Come to me, brother wolf and in Christ's name I command you not to harm me or anybody."

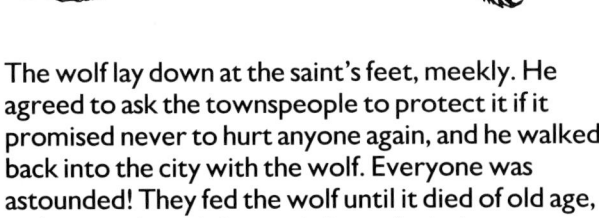

The wolf lay down at the saint's feet, meekly. He agreed to ask the townspeople to protect it if it promised never to hurt anyone again, and he walked back into the city with the wolf. Everyone was astounded! They fed the wolf until it died of old age, and remembered their visit from the holy man.

Another story tells that the saint stopped a boy from selling some doves he had caught in a net. Fearing for their lives, Fancis persuaded him to hand them over and he built nests for them and so they lived among the friars, the companions of Francis.

A Muslim Story

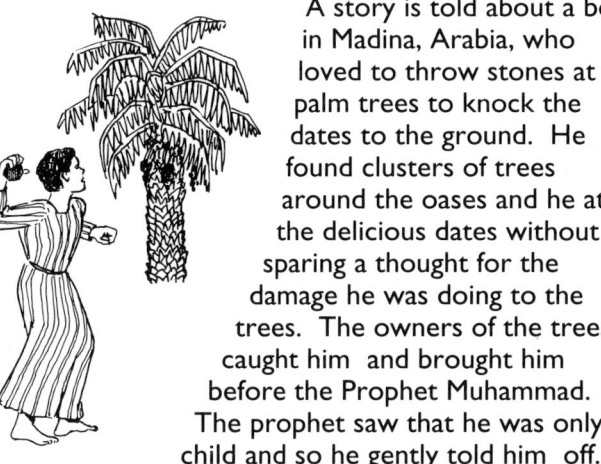

A story is told about a boy in Madina, Arabia, who loved to throw stones at the palm trees to knock the dates to the ground. He found clusters of trees around the oases and he ate the delicious dates without sparing a thought for the damage he was doing to the trees. The owners of the trees caught him and brought him before the Prophet Muhammad. The prophet saw that he was only a child and so he gently told him off. He said, "Don't throw stones at the trees. For if the trees are damaged, they will not bring forth new fruit. Eat the dates that have already fallen to the ground."

A Hindu Story

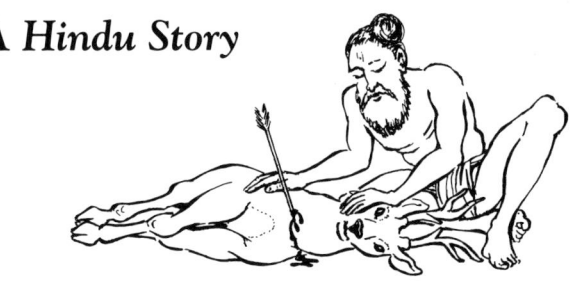

An Indian holy man, Narada Muni, saw a deer lying half dead, with an arrow through it, in agony. Further along the path he saw a boar and a rabbit shot by arrows and in great pain. He went on and found the hunter, who admitted that he enjoyed inflicting pain upon animals before they died. The holy man pleaded with him to stop this cruelty and the hunter was ashamed and convinced of his wrongdoing. He asked Narada Muni how he could find forgiveness. The holy man told him to break his bow and to become one of his disciples. He was sent to live with his wife by the river, in peace, and the holy man helped to provide them with food.

THINGS TO DO

1 Draw a comic strip telling the story of St.Francis' meeting with the wolf.

2 Draw a large date and write in it what you think the moral of the Muslim story is.

3 The Hindu story tells us about animals suffering unnecessary pain at our hands. We experiment on animals to test medicines and cosmetics. Do you think it is right for people to do this? Write down some reasons for and against these experiments.

7 It's the Best! - Exploring Worship Today

When we really enjoy something, we like to spend time being involved with it and thinking about it. We might like many things, but some things are extra special, and, if we are honest, we would find it hard to live without them. They help to make life worth living.

The word 'worship' means that something has 'worth', it is worthwhile. It is good, respected and enjoyed. We worship things that really give us joy, that make our lives worth living!

Some people follow a pop group, buy all their albums, and go to their concerts. They show how much they enjoy their music by dancing, and jumping and singing along. Others might follow a football team, and they dress up in special clothes - hats, scarves, badges, certain colours of jumpers and trousers, to show that they are true fans. Bedroom walls might be covered with film or pop stars, or items to do with sport.

People will give time and money to the thing they worship, and they might dress up in strange ways that they would never dream of doing at any other time! The people below are all worshipping something. What do you think makes their life worth living?

THINGS TO DO

1 Say what 'worship' means, in your own words.

2 Split up into pairs, and talk about the things that you worship. Try to explain why certain things are very special to you.

3 Design a poster about the things that are special to you.

4 Find out how some football supporters and some pop fans dress up to follow their particular team of group. Collect some photographs of this, or draw pictures yourself.

Religious Worship - in a Hindu Temple

These worshippers are Hindus. Believers worship God because they think God is the most special thing in the universe! God is in all things and makes them exist.

Believers worship God to give thanks for the gift of life.

Believers do many things to worship God; they move their bodies; they sing and play music, and decorate their places of worship with beautiful things.

Thanks for Life and Love!   **You're the Greatest!**

Movement   **Music**   **Decoration**

THINGS TO DO

1   Why do religious believers worship God?

2   Look at the drawings above. Do they suggest that worship is dull and formal, or exciting and colourful? Describe the feelings that each of them express for a worshipper.

3   Under the three headings - Movement, Music, and Decoration - draw some pictures to show how a football fan might use these to enthuse about his or her team.

Christian Worship

This is a scene from a Roman Catholic service called *the Mass*. The people recall how Jesus died for them on a cross, and how God raised him again to a new life. It is a celebration of how much these people think God loves them. Bread and wine are blessed and shared out, and these represent the Body and Blood of Jesus.

It is very elaborate - people wear special clothes, especially the priest who leads the worship. There are various movements, decorations, and sounds and smells, here;

The priest dresses in colourful robes, and cup and plate for the bread and wine are made of silver or gold. Candles flicker on the altar.

Words are read out of the Bible, prayers are said, and some hymns are sung.

The bread is placed into people's hands and they eat it.

There is the sweet smell of perfumed incense.

THINGS TO DO

1   Look at the photograph above and list any words that come into your mind.

2   Draw a chart showing how each of the five senses is used in the Mass, labelling SIGHT, TOUCH, TASTE, HEARING, and SMELL.

3   What do you think it would be like to be a part of this worship?

The Christians worshipping in the photo above have a style that is very different from the ceremonial worship of the mass. They are members of a House Church. There are no special clothes or decorations. There is lively music from guitars and the people are moving their bodies. Some are even dancing! These people feel that their worship should be free, relaxed and joyful.

MOVEMENT

Raised hands suggests surrender to God.
Open hands suggests that the worshippers are open to God, welcoming God into their lives.

MUSIC

Various modern instruments will be used, such as guitars, flutes and drums. The songs are short and catchy and they are repeated over and over again. Some people will clap along to the rythmn.

DECORATION

There are no statues, paintings, crosses or candles. The place of worship is plain and simply furnished. There might be a banner, or some words from the Bible.

THINGS TO DO

1   Compare the photograph above with the one of the mass. Do they produce different feelings in you? What do you feel?

2   The place of worship might be plain, but do you think the worship sounds dull? What might give it energy and life?

Places of Worship

All religions have places where people meet for worship. Some are plain and simple, some are very ornate and decorative. They are holy places because they are set apart for prayer and believer's often feel a sense of peace there, though they believe that God is everywhere.

The picture above is a Christian place of worship. It is very quiet, and people come and go, saying their prayers. Candles are lit as a sign of their prayers, and these flicker in the halflight.

Believers do not only worship God in a special building. They pray and praise anywhere. The men in the photograph belong to the Muslim faith. They are saying their prayers outside, in Hyde Park, London. Their prayers involve certain movements of the body, and praises to God in Arabic. Muslims are expected to pray in this way five times a day.

There are some statutes and religious pictures, and the main altar, where the bread and the wine are blessed in the Mass, has a cross and six candles. This is seen as the holiest place in the building, and some of the blessed bread is kept here.

Meal times can be times of worship for some believers. This Jewish family have gathered together to celebrate the Shabbat meal. Shabbat marks the end of the week, and a time of rest from work. The meal is held on Friday evening, and Shabbat continues until Saturday evening.

Prayers are said at the eating and drinking of bread and wine and the lighting of the Shabbat candles:

Blessed are you O Lord our God, King of the Universe, who has sanctified us by thy commandments, and commanded up to kindle the Sabbath light.

THINGS TO DO

1   Visit a place of worship. Then write down what you saw there, and the feelings you experienced during the visit..

2   Design a place of worship - what sort of musical instruments, seating, decoration etc. would you have? Be original - think differently!

8 God?

JACOB'S DREAM
- a story from the Hebrew Bible

Jacob was one of the ancestors of the people of Israel, who probably lived over a thousand years before Jesus was born. There is a story told of him sleeping at Bethel, an ancient holy place in the land of Canaan. In his dreams he felt that God spoke with him, and he saw a vision of angels going up and down a ladder to heaven.

> At sunset he came to a holy place and camped there. He lay down to sleep, resting his head on a stone. He dreamt that he saw a stairway reaching from earth to heaven, with angels going up and coming down on it. And there was the Lord standing beside him. "I am the Lord, the God of Abraham and Isaac," he said "Remember, I will be with you and protect you wherever you go, and I will bring you back to this land. I will not leave you until I have done all that I have promised you." Jacob woke up and said, "The Lord is here! He is in this place and I didn't know it!" He was afraid and said, "What a terrifying place this is! It must be the house of God..."

> Jacob got up early the next morning, took the stone that was under his head and set up up as a memorial. Then he poured olive oil on it to dedicate it to God.

We hear people talk about 'God', but what is God? People say their prayers in public and in private, they sing hymns and worship songs, they bow and kneel and sometimes raise their hands in worship. They teach about God, and sometimes feel that God guides them in life.

Yet God cannot be seen. God is invisible. God cannot be put under a microscope, or in a test-tube, or photographed, or tested in any way with scientific equipment. What is God? Some people wonder if God is real at all, or just a belief in some people's minds.

Some people do not think there is a God, and they are known as *atheists*. Others are not sure, and are called *agnostics*. Those who believe in God are known as *believers* or *theists*.

God is something people disagree about - God is real; God is imaginary; God might or might not be there. Many people in our world do believe in God, and they do things to worship God. Their beliefs are very special to them, and give them comfort and help through life. Whatever your personal feelings about God, it is important to understand what God is supposed to be and to be sensitive to the beliefs of others.

There is a God!

There's no such thing!

I just don't know!

THINGS TO DO

1 What did Jacob see and what promise was given to him?

2 Why do you think that Jacob found the experience 'terrifying'? How does the story make you feel?

3 Make a list of the things that believers do which show that they believe in God.

God isn't up there!

People in ancient times thought that the world was flat, with heaven up above the sky (which was dome shaped) and the Underworld of the dead, or Hell, down below. That is why people still speak about looking up to heaven, or they say that God comes down to us. It is old fashioned picture language that we cannot believe now, word for word.

We know that the Earth is a globe, a planet spinning around the Sun. There is space 'up there', not heaven. Yet many people still believe in God.

Most people do not think of God as a thing out there somewhere, but as an invisible presence, that is everywhere at once. Not just in heaven, not just here, but *everywhere*, and in each one of us.

THINGS TO DO

1   Why do you think people thought of the world in the way shown in the picture above, in the days before telescopes and spaceships?

2   Read the Jacob story again, and see how his dream fits in with how he understood the world.

3   The Bible is full of picture language, saying that God is up there above us, or that he came down to Earth. e.g. read *John 3:31*

4   How do modern people understand God - do they think that, one day, a powerful telescope will find him out in space?

Many believers today think that God is everywhere at once. We should look for God *within* us rather than by looking up beyond the clouds. God is in the *life* that flows through all of us, the *beauty* in a morning sunrise or a dark forest, the *endlessness* of space, the *love* people can show to each other, and the *mystery* of why anything should exist at all.

God is something like 'The Force' in the Star Wars films, a power that is everywhere but cannot be seen.

Believers also feel that God can be prayed to and loved - God is more than a form of spiritual electricity. God is personal, but in a way that is far greater than we are.

Believers say that God cannot be seen in himself, rather like the wind, but God can be seen in things, and in the effect they have on us.

" God can be seen in the beauty of nature.

God can be seen wherever there is love.

God can be seen in a person praying, full of peace. "

THINGS TO DO

1   Do you think that God can be seen in any of the things that are around you? If so, what are they?

2   There are many things that we cannot see that are important. Can you see happiness, for example? Think of some others.

Pictures of God

Shiva's dance

In the Hindu religion, stories are told about different gods, and statues are made of them, but these are really only different parts of the same God. One way Hindus picture God is as Shiva.

A detail from Michaelangelo's Creation of Adam (Sistine Chapel, Rome).

Christians rarely picture God in their places of worship. Sometimes God has been shown as a white-haired old man in the sky. The white hair suggests wisdom, and the age suggests that he is everlasting. Being high up suggests that he is more important than anything else. This is only a picture, though. God cannot be seen!

Christians have pictures of Jesus, his mother Mary and the saints. They think that Jesus shows people what God is like - that he loved us with God's love, which was within him. He and God were one. But God is invisible, and cannot really be pictured. Jesus said:

God is spirit

Jews and Muslims are forbidden to picture God in a painting or statue. They fear that people will worship the picture and forget how great and mysterious God really is. Muslim places of worship may be decorated with stylised arabic writing.

- *The many arms suggest extra power and skill*
- *The dance represents the dance of creation, as God creates life, moving fron one thing to the next.*
- *The circle of fire represents the everlasting nature of God, as a circle goes round and round forever. The fire suggests God's power to destroy and rebuild.*
- *The drum stands for sound, and God's words, or power, that creates.*
- *The flame in Shiva's hand stands for God's power to change and destroy creation.*
- *The demon represents evil and ignorance. Shiva has it underfoot, showing that God is greater than evil.*

Yet this is only a *picture*; God is not actually supposed to look like this.

THINGS TO DO

1   Think of ways in which life can be like a dance. Think of things that are always moving and changing - leaves grow and fall, day follows night. People get up, go our, come back home. Write down some examples of this dance of life.

THINGS TO DO

1   Write about, or draw, the picture that you had of God when you were a child. Explain what the different things in the picture stood for.

2   Make up a new picture, using some of the images that we have talked about in this chapter.

3   What does it mean to say 'God is Spirit'?

Stories about God

Read through these stories and talk about them as a class. What are they trying to say about God?

1 The Little Fish

"Excuse me," said an ocean fish. "You are older than I, so can you tell me where to find this thing they call the ocean?"

"The ocean," said the older fish, "is the thing you are in now."

"Oh, this? But this is water. What I'm seeking is the ocean," said the disappointed fish as he swam away to search elsewhere.

2 The Song of the Bird

The disciples were full of questions about God.

Said the master, "God is the Unknown and the Unknowable. Every statement about him, every answer to your questions, is a distortion of the truth."

The disciples were bewildered. "Then why do you speak about him at all?"

"Why does the bird sing?" said the master.

3 The Boy and the Sea

One day two men were walking by the beach. They saw a little boy running to fill a bucket with water. He ran back to the beach to fill a hole he had dug.

"What are you doing?" asked one of the men.

"Why, I'm trying to put the sea into my hole!" answered the boy.

The two men laughed and walked on.

Walk on!

Many Buddhists, and followers of Taoism, do not talk about God. They talk about the spiritual life, about love, peace and beauty. It is important for us to walk along this path through our lives, being at peace with ourselves, and with one another. Do you think this is the same as believing in God?

YES! NO!

Believers feel that God proves his existence to them in a personal way. It is like falling in love - you cannot prove that you are really in love with someone, but you feel that you are and you act accordingly. Atheists disagree. Love is special, there are wonderful things in life and nature can be beautiful, but they accept the world as it is, without the need for a god to explain it.

"You can't prove there is a God!"

"No, but you can't prove there isn't either! It's a *belief* that means a great deal to many people."

"But I like to deal the things I can see and touch... Where is God?"

"Not everything in life can be worked out like 2+2=4! There are important things we can't see - like love, or joy..."

"So, you can't *prove* you're in love with someone, you just feel that you are..."

"Yes, and believers 'see' God in the wonder of the universe, in acts of love, and when they feel a special presence in prayer, or in a place of worship."

"Isn't all that just in the mind..."

"You can't prove that, and it doesn't seem like it to them..."

THINGS TO DO

1   List some reasons for and against belief in God. Against each of them, try to say how a person with the opposite view might reply.

9 Forever and ever!

Circles

Circles fascinate people. Some mazes are in the form of a circle, and you wind your way into the centre.

People can form circles when dancing; an old form of a circle dance in Britain is the May Pole dance.

The people go in and out of each other in a circle around the pole as they celebrate the birth of spring.

THINGS TO DO

1   Draw a circle and draw in winding paths. One path reaches a small circle at the centre. Draw yourself in this, looking peaceful.

This is like a drawing of your own mind. The paths are the different feelings you have during the day. Your thoughts go this way and that, but deep down, there is the real you.

Circles can also represent things that go on forever. A circle has no beginning and no end - it goes round and round forever.

Circles are used in religion to express the idea of eternity - something going on forever. Think of the haloes around the heads of saints, Jesus, or the gods and goddesses of different faiths.

The steel bangle worn by Sikhs (the *kara*) represents God, who goes on forever. It also represents the unity of all Sikhs in one faith.

Wedding rings represent the love between two people, that they hope will go on and on and on.

Space - the final frontier

Outer space seems vast. Millions and millions of miles separate the planets from one another. The Earth is 93 million miles from the sun. Our solar system with its star (the sun) and planets is a tiny part of the Milky Way, which contains about 100,000 million stars. And the Milky Way is just one of millions of Galaxies that we know of. Space is vast!

> "Space... is big. Really big. You just won't believe how vastly hugely mindbogglingly big it is. I mean you may think it's a long way down the road to the chemist, but that's just peanuts to space... "

> (from *The Hitch Hiker's Guide to the Galaxy*.)

Scientists wonder whether space goes on forever or not. The universe might be infinite - without end. Other scientists think it has limits. The galaxies are all moving apart from each other, possibly after the 'Big Bang', the huge explosion at the start of the universe. Will they move outwards forever, or will they collapse back again? We just do not know.

THINGS TO DO

1 Find out how far away Alpha Centauri is, the nearest star to us.

2 Have you ever looked up at the night sky - at the millions of stars and galaxies? Write down what your feelings as you gazed upwards.

We can see smaller and smaller things, too. Under a microscope, everything looks very different. There are shapes and colours, and things moving that you had no idea of with the naked eye. See if you can guess what these things are:

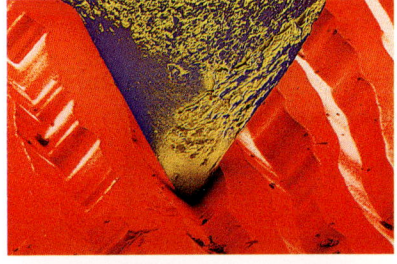

Scientists trace things back to molecules, which are groups of atoms. Atoms are made up of smaller particles. Where does it all end? Can we keep on going smaller and smaller forever?

THINGS TO DO

1 Look at your skin under a microscope. You may want to paint a picture based on what you see, trying to capture the different shapes and colours.

Going round and round!

Look at the picture above. Where does one thing start and another finish? It just seems to go on forever and ever. How does this make you feel?

> **What's the biggest number you can think of?**

Count up the biggest number you can think of. Then add one, then multiply by two... You can never find the largest number. You can go on adding to it, or multiplying it forever, to infinity. Infinity means 'never ending'.

> **What's the smallest number you can think of?**

Think of the smallest number, take away one, and one again, and so on, to infinity.

In mathematics, the letter π stands for 3.333 recurring. This means that there is a never ending string of decimal places. This is confusing, and hard for us to understand. We cannot easily cope with something that goes on forever!

The mathematical symbol for infinity is:

Why do you think this is so?

Something that has no start or finish baffles the human mind. The Moebius strip is a piece of paper folded in such a way that it has no beginning and no end!

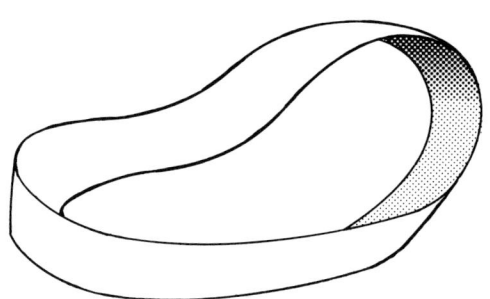

THINGS TO DO

To prove that this is so, make a strip.

1   Take a long strip of paper and twist it, holding both ends together.

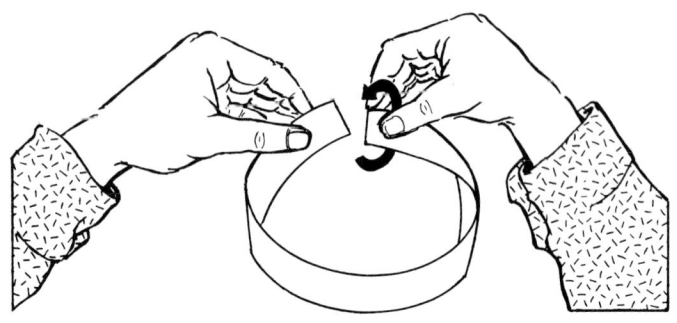

2   Stick the edges together, and then run your finger, or a pencil, along its surface. It has only one side!

42

Nothing that we know lasts forever - everything starts sometime and finishes. An acorn grows into a tall oak, and this whithers and dies. We will all grow old and die one day. A good story comes to an end on the last page.

Even if the whole known universe goes on and on and on, it must have had some kind of beginning, and one day it will come to an end.

We are finite - we start and finish. We cannot imagine anything that is infinite, that just goes on forever.

Believers say that God is infinite. God is a vast mystery that we can never understand. God just is; God had no beginning and will have no end. Nothing made God; God makes things! The Christian New Testament puts it like this:

> Holy, holy, holy, is the Lord God Almighty, who was, who is, and who is to come. (*Revelation* 4:8)

Questions confront us; is there an infinite Spirit; or a universe that stretches out forever, or is there just a series of stars and planets that come and go, and a time when they will all be finished, and nothing at all will exist?

To try to understand how different it would be to be infinite, think of the following things:

Imagine that the more you eat, the more hungry you become, and the emptier your stomach becomes!

Imagine that the longer and faster you run, the easier it gets and you are filled with more and more energy!

Imagine that when you hear a joke, you laugh louder and longer each second as it gets funnier and funnier, without any end to your joy!

THINGS TO DO

1 What does it mean to be finite?

2 If we are finite beings, why do we find it hard to imagine something that is infinite?

3 How do believers answer the question "Who made God?"?

4 Imagine some situations like the ones above. Write about them and draw a picture for each of them.

10 Life after Death

A butterfly breaks out of its chrysalis. Some time before, it was a small, grey caterpillar. It 'died' to one way of life, and started another. Yet, it did not actually die. It just changed from one into the other, in this life.

Can we live again after we die? Many people, though not all, believe that we can, and they have different ideas about what might happen.

The Funeral

Vanessa has just been to Church to say goodbye to her grandfather. She was dressed in new clothes and her mother held her hand tightly all through the service. The minister said how much everybody missed her grandad and then they said some prayers and sang a hymn. Her mother wept a little, and Vanessa felt cold inside. She missed her grandad very much.

Outside, she put some golden and orange flowers on his grave. The sun glistened on them. They smelt beautiful. People did not say very much. They were quiet, and just looked. Some hugged her mum and gave her hand a squeeze.

At home, there were sandwiches and cake, drinks and crisps. Lots of people chatted, uncles and cousins, and people that used to know her grandad. She sat in a corner and looked at a photo of him. Her mind wandered, and she remembered how she used to walk in the park with him, and cuddle up close when he came to visit. Tears dripped down her face. Where had he gone to? It was as though a door had closed, and she could not see him, or touch him, or speak to him anymore.

Later on, her father cuddled her and said that we all had to leave this life sometime. It was sad, but that is how life is. They had loved grandad and they could always remember him. He had lived a long life, and he had given up his old and tired body. His life had gone from it, and was now somewhere else in a new body.

They wept, and cuddled for a long time.

THINGS TO DO

1　Think of the first time you realised what death was. Write a few lines about this.

2　Does death scare you? Why?

3　What different feelings does Vanessa have during the funeral day?

4　Talk as a class about the different views you have about life and death.

Read this story from *Watership Down*, by Richard Adams, a book about rabbits, imagining that they can think and speak like human beings. It is from the end of the book, when Hazel the rabbit has grown very old:

One chilly, blustery morning in March, I cannot tell exactly how many springs later, Hazel was dozing and waking in his burrow. He had spent a good deal of time there lately, for he felt the cold and could not seem to smell or run so well as in days gone by. He had been dreaming in a confused way - something about rain and elder bloom - when he awoke to realise that there was a rabbit lying quietly beside him no doubt some young buck who had come to ask his advice... He raised his head and said, "Do you want to talk to me?"

"Yes, that's what I've come for," replied the other. "You know me, don't you?"

"Yes, of course," said Hazel, hoping he would be able to remember his name in a moment. Then he saw that in the darkness of the burrow, the stranger's ears were shining with a faint, silver light. "Yes, My Lord," he said. "Yes, I know you."

"You've been feeling tired", said the stranger, "but I can do something about that... If you're ready, we might go along now."

They went out past the young sentry, who paid the visitor no attention... It seemed to Hazel that he would not be needing his body any more, so he left it lying on the edge of the ditch, but stopped for a moment to watch his rabbits and to try to get used to the extraordinary feeling that strength and speed were flowing inexhaustibly out of him into their sleek young bodies and healthy senses.

"You needn't worry about them", said his companion. "They'll be alright - and thousands like them. If you'll come along, I'll show you what I mean."

He reached the top of the bank in a single powerful leap. Hazel followed; and together they slipped away, running easily down through the wood, where the first primroses were beginning to bloom.

THINGS TO DO

1 How does this passage make you feel?

2 Say, in your own words, what you think happens in the story.

3 Do you think this story would have helped Vanessa, the girl you read about at the beginning of this chapter? Does death seem something to be scared of in the story?

4 Either draw the scene from the story where Hazel looks at his old tired body, or the scene where he sees the rabbit glowing with light in the burrow.

Resurrection

There are different ideas about what form the after-life might take. We are going to look at two of them: resurrection and reincarnation.

The two pictures above show Jesus dying on a cross and then rising into a glorious new life. Christians believe that his life did not end when the Romans tortured him and nailed him to a cross; God raised him to a new life. He was transformed and lives spiritually in a new body. The books about him in the Bible, the Gospels, tell how he appeared to his first followers and special friends to assure them that he lived, and that God would raise them after they died.

Many people take comfort from this belief. This idea of leaving this life and being raised to a new one in the afterlife is called RESURRECTION.

This means that we leave our old bodies, as worn out and finished with, but our spirits are raised in new bodies that are not flesh and blood but new ways of being alive, obeying different laws of physics.

We leave this earth and live in the after-life, wherever that is. It is a mystery.

Jews, Christians and Muslims believe in resurrection.

Resurrection is an idea about what happens when you die, but there are many 'little resurrections' happening all around us, here and now.

Whenever something sad and miserable changes into something happy and joyful, a little resurrection has happened. Something old has been raised into a new life.

RESURRECTION IS ...

Two friends made up after having a row.

A desert is made fertile by farmers and there is plenty of food for the people.

THINGS TO DO

1 What do Christians think happened to Jesus after he died?

2 Look at the two paintings above. What words suggest the difference between them.

3 Look at the picture of Jesus rising. What would it have felt like to have been there?

4 Think up ideas for 'Resurrection is ...' and write these down, perhaps with drawings or photographs cut out of magazines.

Reincarnation

The Dalai Lama, the Buddhist leader of the people of Tibet, was chosen while still a child. When the previous Dalai Lama died, monks went in search of a boy of a suitable age who might be his reincarnation. When shown special items worn by the previous Dalai Lama, he put them on in the correct manner. The monks took this as a sign that he was his reincarnation.

The idea of reincarnation is not something that we can prove scientifically. Stories of people claiming to remember previous lives are often very mysterious, and there may be other explanations for them: they might be imagining it, or remembering something they read in a book long ago. Those who believe in reincarnation, think that everything they do in this life has an effect, for good or ill, on the life of the world in the future, and that this goes on, even after their own death.

The picture above is a Buddhist wheel of life. Life is like a wheel, and our position on it is constantly changing. Hindus, Buddhists and Sikhs believe in REINCARNATION - that after we die we may take on another life on earth, as another person, or some other creature. What we are reborn as depends upon our deeds in former lives, and our 'score' is known as our *karma*. The goal is to escape from the endless cycle of dying and being born, and to reach something like heaven, a union with God, or a state of perfect peace. Buddhists call this Nirvana. Notice on the wheel of life that a path leads out of the wheel and towards an image of the Buddha.

This is a passage from the Hindu holy book, the Gita:

> As a man leaves an old garment and puts on one that is new, the spirit leaves his mortal body and then puts on one that is new.

Some people claim to remember scenes from a past life, perhaps under hypnosis. We all have the experience of 'deja-vu' sometimes, when we think we have been somewhere before but cannot remember when.

THINGS TO DO

1 Draw a wheel of life. You may want to divide it into the stages of birth, growing up, growing old and dying.

2 If you were to be reborn, what would you want to come back as? Does your choice say something about the way you behave and the things you like now? Talk about this in class.

3 Think of an experience of 'deja-vu' that you have had, or have heard about. Write a few lines about it. How did you feel?

4 Write a sentence saying what you think the difference is between RESURRECTION and REINCARNATION.

Teacher's Notes

Chapter 1

Suggest that the class read *The Wizard of Earthsea* by Ursula Le Guin. In this story, a young boy, Sparrowhawk, is trained by Wizards. He is tempted to use spells he cannot control, and he unleashes a shadow-beast that threatens to destroy everything. He finally meets the beast in the last chapter. It vanishes when he speaks its name - his name! When he faces up to his own evil, it is conquered.

Chapter 2

The theme of journeying could be extended to study the plight of refugees, perhaps with a sponsored activity to raise money to help. Organisations to contact about this:
OXFAM, 274 Banbury Road, Oxford, OX2 7DZ
Christian Aid, PO Box 1, London, SW98BH
CAFOD, 2 Garden Close, Stockwell, London, SW9 9TY

Chapter 4

Following a discussion of 'walls' and 'barriers', the class could think of things that divide people, both globally and personally. These could be written up on a roll of wallpaper stretched across the room, and pupils could be invited to break through it.For more information about Corrymeela, contact: Corrymeela Community, Ballycastle, Co.Antrin, BT54 6QU, N.Ireland

Chapter 5

You could read and discuss passages from a book about Mother Teresa (e.g. *Something Beautiful for God* by Malcolm Muggeridge, her thoughts pp64-79 or the interview pp83-121). Some pupils might be able to enter imaginatively into the situation of a dying person who has been brought in off the streets and is being cared for by one of the Sisters. They could write a letter to a Sister, expressing gratitude for this.It might be possible to visit a local home for the Elderly, perhaps establishing links as part of a Community Service programme. A Warden from a Home for the Elderly (or local sheltered accommodation) could be invited to come and speak to pupils about his or her work.For further information on homelessness:
Shelter, 157 Waterloo Road, London, SE1 8UO
Catholic Housing Aid Agency, 137 Holland Road, London, W14
Salvation Army, 101 Victoria Street, London, EC4P 4EP

Chapter 6

To organise a Green project for your locality, you could contact Friends of the Earth for ideas. Their address: Friends of the Earth, 26-28 Underwood Street, London N1 7JQ. Pupils could create a display board with information about helping to protect species. For information about whales, contact: The Whale and Dolphin Conservation Society, 20 West Lea Rd., Weston, Bath, BA1 3RL.

To follow up the Hindu story about kindness to animals, pupils could be encouraged to find out more about the work of the RSPCA. Their address is: RSPCA, Causeway, Horsham, West Sussex, RH12 1HG

Chapter 7

You could arrange a 'worship corner' in the classroom, where pupils could display objects of special value or significance for them.Videos and cassettes of modern praise songs and charismatic worship are available, to give pupils a feel for this sort of worship.You could arrange visits to local places of worship, followed by a 'brainstorming' session to check out pupils' responses. They could also write accounts of things that seemed striking or important. Members of faiths who say special prayers at home might be invited to talk to the class. Perhaps they could bring in any special objects (e.g. Shabbat candles).

Chapter 8

You could ask how many pupils in the class hold views like those on page 36 - those who believe in God, those who do not, and those who don't know. In any discussion, some pupils might wish to abstain from sharing their views, and sensitivity is needed over this. Pupils could be encouraged to describe how they pictured God when they were younger, and what certain things in their pictures stood for.

Following the idea of Shiva's cosmic dance on page 38, you could read the account of the creation of Narnia in *The Magician's Nephew* by C.S.Lewis (chapter 9). The land is created by Aslan's song.

Chapters 25 and 28 of Douglas Adams' *The Hitch Hiker's Guide to the Galaxy* deal with the computer 'Deep Thought' and the attempt to find the meaning of 'life, the universe and everything'.

Chapter 9

The items shown on page 41 seen under the false colour scanning electron micrograph are: (upper left) a diamond stylus travelling through the grooves of an LP record; (lower left) part of a strip of velcro fastener - as the two types of nylon material come together, the hooks catch the loops; (right) a single strand of cotton passing through the eye of a needle.

Chapter 10

Read the account of the death of Aslan the Lion in chapter 14 of C.S.Lewis' *The Lion, The Witch and the Wardrobe*, and then his resurrection in chapter 15. Compare these stories with the accounts of the death and resurrection of Jesus.